The Book of John Whitmer

By John Whitmer

Copyright © 2021 Lamp of Trismegistus. All rights reserved. No part of this publication may be reproduced or transmitted in any form or by any means, electronic or mechanical, including photocopying, recording, or by any information storage and retrieval system, without permission in writing from Lamp of Trismegistus. Reviewers may quote brief passages.

ISBN: 978-1-63118-554-0

*Mormon History
Series*

Other Books in this Series and Related Titles

Pearl of Great Price by Joseph Smith (978-1-63118-539-7)

The Angel of the Prairies or A Dream of the Future: Mormon History Series
By Elder Parley Parker Pratt (978-1-63118-541-0)

A Manuscript on Far West by Reed Peck (978-1-63118-544-1)

Private Diary of Joseph Smith 1832-1834 (978-1-63118-546-5)

The Story of Mormonism by James E Talmage (978-1-63118-543-4)

Interesting Account of Several Remarkable Visions: Mormon History Series
By Orson Pratt (978-1-63118-553-3)

An Address to All Believers in Christ Elder David Whitmer (978-1-63118-545-8)

The Philosophy of Mormonism by James E Talmage (978-1-63118-542-7)

The Book of Abraham: Mormon History by George Reynolds (978-1-63118-540-3)

The Testament of Abraham by Abraham (978-1-63118-441-3)

The Book of the Watchers by Enoch (978-1-63118-416-1)

The Testament of Moses by Moses (978-1-63118-440-6)

Times and Seasons Volume 1, Numbers 1-3 (978-1-63118-555-7)

Times and Seasons Volume 1, Numbers 4-6 (978-1-63118-556-4)

The Evening and Morning Star Volume 1, Numbers 1 & 2 (978-1-63118-547-2)

The Evening and Morning Star Volume 1, Numbers 3 & 4 (978-1-63118-548-9)

The Evening and Morning Star Volume 1, Numbers 5 & 6 (978-1-63118-549-6)

The Evening and Morning Star Volume 1, Numbers 7 & 8 (978-1-63118-550-2)

The Evening and Morning Star Volume 1, Numbers 9 & 10 (978-1-63118-551-9)

The Evening and Morning Star Volume 1, Numbers 11 & 12 (978-1-63118-552-6)

Audio Versions are also available on Audible, Amazon and Apple

Other Books in this Series and Related Titles

The Hidden Mysteries of Christianity by Annie Besant (978–1–63118–534–2)

American Indian Freemasonry by A C Parker (978-1-63118-460-4)

Rosicrucian Rules, Secret Signs, Codes and Symbols by various (978-1-63118-488-8)

History and Teachings of the Rosicrucians by W W Westcott &c (978-1-63118-487-1)

Freemasonry and the Egyptian Mysteries by C. W. Leadbeater (978-1-63118-456-7)

The Secrets of Enoch by Enoch (978-1-63118-449-9)

The Psalms of Solomon by King Solomon (978-1-63118-439-0)

The Historic, Mythic and Mystic Christ by Annie Besant (978–1–63118–533–5)

The Book of Parables by Enoch (978-1-63118-429-1)

Some Deeper Aspects of Masonic Symbolism by A E Waite (978-1-63118-461-1)

Masonic Symbolism of King Solomon's Temple by A Mackey &c (978-1-63118-442-0)

The Old Past Master by Carl H Claudy (978-1-63118-464-2)

Book of Dreams by Enoch (978-1-63118-437-6)

The Book of Astronomical Secrets by Enoch (978-1-63118-443-7)

Masonic Symbolism of the Apron & the Altar by various (978-1-63118-428-4)

The Book of Wisdom of Solomon by King Solomon (978-1-63118-502-1)

Masonic Symbolism of Easter and the Christ in Masonry (978-1-63118-434-5)

The Odes of Solomon by King Solomon (978-1-63118-503-8)

Ancient Mysteries and Secret Societies by M P Hall (978-1-63118-410-9)

The Golden Verses of Pythagoras: Five Translations (978-1-63118-479-6)

A Few Masonic Sermons by A. C. Ward &c (978-1-63118-435-2)

Audio versions are also available on Audible, Amazon and Apple

Table of Contents

The Book of John Whitmer

Title Page...7

Chapter 1...9
Chapter 2...15
Chapter 3...17
Chapter 4...19
Chapter 5...21
Chapter 6...23
Chapter 7...27
Chapter 8...29
Chapter 9...31
Chapter 10...37
Chapter 11...45
Chapter 12...57
Chapter 13...61
Chapter 14...63
Chapter 15...67
Chapter 16...69
Chapter 17...75
Chapter 18...77
Chapter 19...79

THE BOOK OF JOHN WHITMER

A portion of
The Book of John Whitmer Kept by Commandment

Written by John Whitmer, 1831-1838.

Being an History of the Church of Jesus Christ
from 1831-1838

taken from
John Whitmer, "The Book of John Whitmer Kept by Commandment," typescript by Pauline Hancock, BYU-A.

Holograph is located in RLDS Archives.
(D&C references that are different in the LDS and RLDS editions of the Doctrine and Covenants are noted.)

THE BOOK OF JOHN WHITMER
KEPT BY COMMANDMENT
CHAPTER 1

I shall proceed to continue this record, being commanded of the Lord and Savior Jesus Christ, to write the things that transpire in this Church (inasmuch as they come to my knowledge,) in these last days. It is now June the twelfth, one thousand eight hundred and thirty one years, since the coming of our Lord and Savior in the flesh. Not many days after my brethren, Oliver Cowdery, Peter Whitmer, Jr., Parley P. Pratt, and Ziba Peterson: received a commandment of the Lord, through Joseph Smith, Jr., to take their journey to the Lamanites and preach the Gospel of our Lord and Savior, among them, and establish the Church of Christ among them. They journeyed as far west as the state of Ohio, and through the divine influences of the Holy Spirit, by the assistance of the Lord, they built a branch of the Church, in Geauga Co., state of Ohio, which consisted of about one hundred and thirty members.

And now it came to pass, that before they proceeded, on their journey from this place, there was a man whose name was Sidney Rigdon, he having been an instrument in the hand of the Lord of doing much good. He was in search of truth, consequently he received the fullness of the gospel with gladness of heart, even the Book of Mormon, it being what he was in search after, notwithstanding it was some days before he obtained a witness from the Lord, of the truth of his work. After several days the Lord heard his cries, and answered his prayers, and by vision showed to him that this emanated from Him and must remain, it being the fullness of the gospel of Jesus Christ, first unto the Gentiles and then unto the Jews.

Now it came to pass, after Sidney Rigdon, was received into this Church, that he was ordained an elder, under the hands of Oliver

Cowdery. He having much anxiety to see Joseph Smith, Jr., the Seer whom the Lord had raised up in these last days. Therefore he took his journey to the state of New York, where Joseph resided.

There was another man whose name is Edward Partridge who was also desirous, to see the Seer, therefore, he accompanied Sidney, and journeyed with him, to behold this man of God, even Joseph Smith, Jr., he being desirous to know the truth of these things: But not having confidence enough to inquire at the hand of God. Therefore he sought testimony of man, and he obtained it, and received the truth and obeyed the divine requirements and was also ordained an elder unto the Church, to preach repentance and remission of sins, unto this idolatrous generation. Wherefore, after Sidney Rigdon had been at Palmyra a few days he proclaimed the gospel, in those regions round about, at which the people stood trembling and amazed, so powerful were his words, and some obeyed the gospel and came forth out of the water, rejoicing with joy which is unspeakable and full of glory. From thence he journeyed to Fayette, where Joseph lived, and there he also proclaimed the gospel in the regions round about and there were numbers added. Now in those days Sidney Rigdon was desirous to have the Seer enquire of the Lord, to know what the will of the Lord was concerning him. Accordingly Joseph enquired of the Lord, and these are the words that were spoken to him: (LDS D&C 35, RLDS D&C 34.)

Now after the Lord had made known what he wanted that his servant Sidney should do, he went to writing the things which the Lord showed unto his servant the Seer. The Lord made known, some of the hidden things of his kingdom; for he unfolded, the prophecy of Enoch the seventh from Adam. After they had written this prophecy, the Lord spoke to them again and gave further directions: (D&C 37.)

After the above directions were received, Joseph and Sidney went to the several churches preaching and prophesying wherever they went, and greatly strengthened the churches that were built unto the Lord. Joseph prophesied saying: God is about to destroy this generation, and Christ will descend from heaven in power and great glory, with all the holy angels with him, to take vengeance upon the wicked, and they that know not God. Sidney preached the gospel and proved his words from the holy prophets: and so powerful were their words, that the people who heard them speak were amazed, and trembled, and knew not whereunto this thing would grow. The adversary of all righteousness being crafty, and beguiled the people, and stirred them up to anger against the words spoken, and has blinded their eyes, and is leading them down to darkness, misery and woe. This generation abounds in ignorance, superstition, selfishness, idolatry, and priestcraft, for this generation is truly led by priests, even hireling priests, whose god is the substance of this world's goods, which waxeth old and is beginning to fade away: who look for their hire every one from his quarter.

Because of the abominations that are abroad in the world, it is hard for those who receive the fullness of the gospel, and come into the new and everlasting covenant, to get clear of the traditions of their forefathers: and are to be made to believe the commandments that came forth in these last days for the upbuilding of the kingdom of God, and the salvation of those who believe.

The time had now come for the general conference to be held. Which was the first of January 1831, and according to this appointment the Saints assembled themselves together. After transacting the necessary business, Joseph the Seer addressed the congregation and exhorted them to stand fast, looking forward considering the end of their salvation. The solemnities of eternity rested on the congregation and having previously received a revelation to go to Ohio, they desired to know somewhat more concerning this matter. Therefore, the Seer enquired of the Lord in the presence of the whole congregation, and thus came the word of the Lord saying: (see D&C 38.)

After the Lord had manifested the above words, through Joseph the Seer, there were some divisions among the congregations, some would not receive the above as the word of the Lord: but that Joseph had invented it himself to deceive the people that in the end he might get gain. Now this was because, their hearts were not right in the sight of the Lord, for they wanted to serve God and man; but our Savior has declared that it was impossible to do so.

The conference was now closed, and the Lord had manifested his will to his people. Therefore they made preparations to journey to the Ohio, with their wives, and children and all that they possessed, to obey the commandment of the Lord. After these things were done Joseph and Sidney went to Colesville to do the will of the Lord in that part of the land and to strengthen the disciples in that part of the vineyard, and preach the gospel to a hardened and a wicked people; and it is fearful that they are all delivered over to hardness of heart and blindness of (mind), so that they cannot be brought to repentance. For when Sidney and the revelator arrived there, they held prayer meetings among the disciples, and they also held public meetings, but it was all in vain; they threatened to kill them. Therefore, they knew that they were not fit for the kingdom of God, and well nigh ripe for destruction. The Spirit of the Lord fell upon Sidney, and he spoke with boldness, and he preached the gospel in its purity; but they laughed him to scorn, he being filled, with the Holy Spirit, he cried aloud, "O ye heavens give ear and ye angels attend, I bear witness in the name of Jesus Christ that this people is sealed up to everlasting destruction." And immediately he left them and escaped out of their hands. And his enemies were astonished and amazed at the doctrines which he preached, for they taught as men having authority and not as hireling priests.

After Joseph and Sidney returned from Colesville to Fayette. The Lord manifested himself to Joseph the Revelator and gave commandment for me to go to Ohio, and carry the commandments and revelations, with me, to comfort and strengthen my brethren in that land. The disciples had increased in numbers about three hundred. But the enemy of all righteousness had got hold of some of those who professed to be his followers, because they had not sufficient knowledge to detect him in all of his devices. He took a notion to blind the minds of some of the weaker ones, and made them think that an angel of the Lord appeared to them and showed them writings on the outside cover of the Bible, and on parchment, which flew through the air, and on the back of their hands, and many such foolish and vain things--others lost their strength, and some slid on the floor, and such like maneuvers, which proved greatly to the injury of the cause.

The Lord also worked, and many embraced the work, and the honest in heart stood firm and immovable. It was very necessary that this people should have instructions, and learn to discern between the things of God and the works of Satan. For the inhabitants of the earth knew nothing of the working of the spirit of the Lord, in these days.

CHAPTER 2

About these days Joseph and Sidney arrived at Kirtland to the joy and satisfaction of the Saints. The disciples had all things common, and were going to destruction very fast as to temporal things; for they considered from reading the scripture that what belonged to a brother, belonged to any of the brethren. Therefore they would take each other's clothes and other property and use it without leave which brought on confusion and disappointments, for they did not understand the scripture. After Joseph lived there a few days the word of the Lord came saying: (See D&C 41.)

Behold, after this revelation was received the elders were called together, and united in mighty power; and were agreed, as touching the reception of the law. Therefore, thus saith the Lord: (See D&C 42. Portions of this section following RLDS D&C 42:19 were not quoted in this history).

CHAPTER 3

After the above law or revelation was received, the elders went forth to proclaim repentance according to commandment, and there were members added to the Church. The Bishop Edward Partridge visited the Church in its several branches, there were some that would not receive the law. The time has not yet come that the law can be fully established, for the disciples live scattered abroad and are not organized, our numbers are small and the disciples untaught, consequently they understand not the things of the kingdom. There were some of the disciples who were flattered into the Church because they thought that all things were to be common, therefore they thought to glut themselves upon the labors of others.

About these days there was a woman by the name of Hubble who professed to be a prophetess of the Lord and professed to have many revelations, and knew the Book of Mormon was true, and that she should become a teacher in the Church of Christ. She appeared very sanctimonious and deceived some who were not able to detect her in her hypocrisy: others however had the spirit of discernment, and her follies and abominations were made manifest. The Lord gave revelation that the Saints might not be deceived which reads as follows: (See LDS D&C 43, RLDS D&C 44.)

After this commandment was received, the saints came to understanding on this subject, and unity and harmony prevailed throughout the Church of God: and the Saints began to learn wisdom, and treasure up knowledge which they learned from the word of God, and by experience as they advanced in the way of eternal life.

And Joseph Smith the Seer continued the translation of the holy scriptures. And the word of the Lord came to Joseph Smith, Jr.: saying: (See D&C 44.)

The translations continued: And the elders were sent for according to preceding revelation.

March 4, 1831. This was a day appointed for a general conference, from whence the elders were sent forth to preach the gospel and many were added of such as were determined to be saved.

About this time some were sick of various diseases, and were healed by the power which was in them through Jesus Christ. There was a tradition among some of the disciples, that those who obeyed the covenant in the last days, would never die: but by experience, they have learned to the contrary.

In those days the Lord blessed his disciples greatly, and he gave revelation after revelation, which contained doctrine, instructions, and prophecies: The word of the Lord came to the seer as follows: (See D&C 45.)

Some of the elders returned from their missions to gain some rest and instructions. They rehearsed some of the wickedness which they had seen among the generations: while they were proclaiming the gospel and warning the people, some would cry false prophets, false christ, etc. Some would receive the word gladly until their priests would cry delusion! delusion!! for this generation abounds with priests, which they have heaped up unto themselves, and every one is teaching for hire: consequently everyone is looking for his gain from his quarter. They will persecute the disciples, and cause their followers to do likewise. Out of the mixed multitude some obey the gospel of peace and bring forth fruit some an hundredfold.

The Lord is pouring forth some of his judgments, in token of the last days. An earthquake in China destroyed about one million of souls. But judgments in these days as in former days seem to harden men, until it is too late to repent.

CHAPTER 4

John Murdock and others held a meeting in the city of Cleveland, Ohio, in the Masonic Hall by the request of some of the citizens of said city. An opportunity which some sought to bring out their evil designs. Elder Murdock addressed the congregation on the subject of the gospel; and warned the inhabitants of that place to flee the wrath to come. Others followed him, and while they were yet speaking one of the congregation came toward the stand and kneeled down and began to pray, a sign to the banditti to begin their abuse. At this time they began to blow out the candles and throw ink stands and books, etc. at the speaker and one of the brethren prayed that the Lord would stop the utterance of the fellow that came and kneeled at the stand, he became silent and could not rise from his knees for sometime, because of the prayer of faith.

In the beginning of the Church, while yet in her infancy, the disciples used to exclude unbelievers, which caused some to marvel, and converse of this matter because of the things that are written in the Book of Mormon. Therefore the Lord deigned to speak on this subject, that his people might come to understanding and said that he had always given to his elders to conduct all meetings as they were led by the Spirit. (See D&C 46.) [Revelation is omitted from the text.]

CHAPTER 5

The time drew near for the brethren from the state of New York to arrive at Kirtland, Ohio. And some had supposed that it was the place of gathering even the place of the New Jerusalem spoken of in the Book of Mormon, according to the visions and revelations received in the last days. There was no preparation made for the reception of the Saints from the East. The bishop being anxious to know something concerning the matter. Therefore the Lord spake unto Joseph Smith, Jr., as follows: (See LDS D&C 48, RLDS D&C 46.)

CHAPTER 6

I returned from Nelson, Ohio, where I and Lyman Wight had built a branch of the Church of Christ. I was appointed by the voice of the elders to keep the Church Record. Joseph Smith, Jr., said unto me you must also keep the Church history. I would rather not do it but observed that the will of the Lord be done, and if he desires it, I desire that he would manifest it through Joseph the Seer. And thus came the word of the Lord: (See D&C 47.)

Oliver Cowdery has written the commencement of the Church history, commencing at the time of the finding of the plates, up to June 12th, 1831. From this date I have written the things that I have written, and they are a mere sketch of the things that have transpired, they are however all that seemed to me wisdom to write many things happened that are to be lamented, because of the weakness and instability of man. The devil having a great hold on the hearts of the children of men, and the foolish traditions of our fathers, is to be lamented, for they count themselves the children of wisdom, and great knowledge, in consequence of which, the fulness of the gospel finds its way to but few of the hearts of this generation. Although their hearts must be penetrated, whether they will hear or whether they will forbear.

Permit me here to remark, that David Whitmer, Oliver Cowdery, and Martin Harris, were the Three Witnesses, whose names are attached to the book of Mormon according to the prediction of the Book, who knew and saw, for a surety, into whose presence the angel of God came and showed them the plates, the ball, the directors, etc. And also other witnesses even eight viz: Christian Whitmer, Jacob Whitmer, John Whitmer, and Peter Whitmer Jr., Hiram Page, Joseph Smith, Hyrum Smith, and Samuel H. Smith, are the men to whom Joseph Smith, Jr., showed the plates, these witnesses names go forth also of the truth of this work in the last days. To the convincing or condemning of this generation in the last days.

Some of the brethren arrived from the state of New York, Samuel H. Smith and Orson Pratt, who were prospered on their journey. The disciples increased daily, and miracles were wrought, such as healing the sick, casting out devils, and the Church grew and multiplied in numbers, grace, and knowledge.

Leman Copley one of the disciples, who was formerly a Shaker Quaker, he was anxious that some of the elders should go to his former brethren and preach the gospel. He also feared to be ordained to preach himself, and desired that the Lord should direct in this and all matters, and thus saith the Lord: (See D&C 49.)

The above-named brethren went and proclaimed according to revelation given to them, but the Shakers hearkened not to their words, and received not the gospel that time; for they were bound up in tradition and priestcraft, and thus they are led away with foolish and vain imaginations.

For a perpetual memory, to the shame and confusion of the devil--permit me, to say a few things, respecting the proceedings of some of those who were disciples, and some remain among us, and will, and have come from under the error and enthusiasm, which they had fallen.

Some had visions and could not tell what they saw. Some would fancy to themselves that they had the sword of Laban, and would wield it as expert as a light dragoon, some would act like an Indian in the act of scalping, some would slide or scoot on the floor, with the rapidity of a serpent, which termed sailing in the boat to the Lamanites, preaching the gospel. And many other vain and foolish maneuvers, that are unmeaning, and unprofitable to mention. Thus the devil blinded the eyes of some good and honest disciples. I write these things to show how ignorant and undiscerning children are and how easy mankind is led astray notwithstanding the things of God that are written, concerning his kingdom.

These things grieved the servants of the Lord, and some conversed together on this subject, and others came in and we were at Joseph Smith Jr. the Seers, and made it a matter of consultation, for many would not turn from their folly, unless God would give a revelation, therefore, the Lord spoke to Joseph saying: (See D&C 50.)

CHAPTER 7

About these days the disciples arrived from state of New York to this place Kirtland, state of Ohio. They had some difficulty because of some that did not continue faithful, who denied the truth and turned into fables.

June 3, 1831, a general conference was called, and a blessing promised, if the elders were faithful, and humble before him. Therefore, the elders assembled from the East and the West, from the North and the South. And also many members. Conference was opened by prayer and exhortation by Joseph Smith, Jr., the Revelator. After the business of the Church was attended to according to the covenants. The Lord made manifest to Joseph that it was necessary that such of the elders as were considered worthy, should be ordained to the High Priesthood.

The spirit of the Lord fell upon Joseph in an unusual manner. And prophesied that John the Revelator was then among the ten tribes of Israel who had been led away by Salmanasar King of Israel [should be Assyria], to prepare them for their return, from their long dispersion, to again possess the land of their fathers. He prophesied many more things that I have not written. After he had prophesied he laid his hands upon Lyman Wight [and ordained him] to the High Priesthood after the Holy Order of God. And the spirit fell upon Lyman, and he prophesied, concerning the coming of Christ, he said that there were some in the congregation that should live until the Savior should descend from heaven, with a shout, with all the holy angels with him. He said the coming of the Savior should be, like; the sun rising in the east, and will cover the whole earth, so with the coming of the Son of man be, yea, he will appear in his brightness and consume all before him. And the hills will be laid low, and the valleys be exalted; and the crooked be made straight; and the rough smooth. And some of my brethren shall suffer martyrdom, for the sake of the religion of Jesus Christ, and seal the testimony of Jesus with their blood.

He saw the heavens opened, and the Son of man sitting on the right hand of the Father. Making intercession for his brethren, the Saints. He said that God would work a work in these last days that tongue cannot express, and the mind is not capable to conceive. The glory of the Lord shone around.

At the conference these were ordained to the high priesthood, namely, Lyman Wight, Sidney Rigdon, John Murdock, Reynolds Cahoon, Harvey Whitlock and Hyrum Smith [they] were ordained by Joseph Smith, Jr., except Sidney Rigdon.

The following by Lyman Wight by commandment. Parley P. Pratt, Thomas B. Marsh, Isaac Morley, Edward Partridge, Joseph Wakefield, Ezra Thayer, Martin Harris, Ezra Booth, who denied the faith, Harvey Whitlock denied the faith, also Joseph Wakefield, Joseph Smith, Sen., Joseph Smith, Jr., [and] John Whitmer. The bishop then proceeded and blessed the above named and others by the laying on of hands. Isaac Morley and John Correll [Corrill] were ordained as bishop's counsellors to Edward Partridge.

Joseph Smith, Jr., prophesied the day previous that the man of sin should be revealed. While the Lord poured out his spirit upon his servants, the devil took a notion, to make known his power, he bound Harvey Whitlock and John Murdock so that they could not speak, and others were affected but the Lord showed to Joseph the Seer, the design of the thing, he commanded the devil in the name of Christ and he departed to our joy and comfort.

Therefore a part of the revelation given at Fayette, New York, was fulfilled. The churches of the state of New York had moved to Ohio, with their wives and their children, and all their substance, some purchased farms others rented, and thus they situated themselves as convenient as they could. The day being now far spent and the conference was adjourned.

CHAPTER 8

June 6, 1831. Received a revelation what to do. (See D&C 52.)

After this revelation was received those elders were making all possible speed who were called to go according to commandment to fill their missions in their several courses.

At this time the Church at Thompson, Ohio, was involved in difficulty, because of the rebellion of Leman Copley. Who would not do as he had previously agreed. Which thing confused the whole Church and finally the Lord spoke to Joseph Smith, Jr., the Prophet saying: (See D&C 54.)

After some of the elders had left and the time for Joseph Smith Jr. and others to leave. Some of those who had been commanded to take their journey speedily, that some had denied the faith, and turned from the truth. And the Church at Thompson, Ohio, had not done according to the will of the (Lord): Therefore, before Joseph and his company left thus came the word of the Lord; saying: (D&C 56.)

The Church at Thompson made all possible haste to leave for Missouri, and left and none of their enemies harmed them. The Church at Chardon, Ohio, was also anxious to take their journey to Missouri, and by much teasing they obtained a permit to take their journey.

CHAPTER 9

There was much trouble and unbelief among those who call themselves disciples of Christ: some apostatized, and became enemies to the cause of God, and persecuted the Saints.

Now after the elders that were commanded to go to Missouri had arrived, they held a conference upon that land according to revelation given in a preceding commandment. And thus they rejoiced together upon the land of Zion. And offered their sacraments and oblations unto the Lord, for his mercy and goodness which endureth for ever.

When they had held their sacrament meetings, and the laying of the foundation of the City, and cornerstone of the temple, the Lord gave commandments to return.

I here give a copy of the proceedings of the laying of the first logs of the city of Zion. As written by Oliver Cowdery:

"After many struggles and afflictions, being persecuted by our enemies, we received intelligence by letter from our brethren; who were at the east. That Brother Joseph and Sidney, and many other elders, were commanded to take their journey to this land, the land of Missouri. Which was promised unto us should be the land of the inheritance of the Saints, and the place of the gathering in these last days. Which intelligence cheered our hearts, and caused us to rejoice exceedingly. And by the special protection of the Lord, Brother Joseph Smith, Jr., and Sidney Rigdon, in company with eight other elders, with the Church from Colesville, New York, consisting of about sixty souls, arrived in the month of July and by revelation the place was made known where the temple shall stand, and the city should commence. And by commandment twelve of us assembled ourselves together, viz., Elder Joseph Smith, Jr., the Seer, Oliver Cowdery, Sidney Rigdon, Newel Knight, William W. Phelps, and Ezra Booth who denied the faith.

"On the 2nd day of August 1831, Brother Sidney Rigdon stood up and asked saying: Do you receive this land for the land of your inheritance with thankful hearts from the Lord? answer from all, we do. Do you pledge yourselves to keep the laws of God on this land, which you never have kept in your own lands? we do. Do you pledge yourselves to see that others of your brethren who shall come hither do keep the laws of God? we do. After prayer he arose and said, I now pronounce this land consecrated and dedicated to the Lord for a possession and inheritance for the Saints (in the name of Jesus Christ having authority from him.) And for all the faithful servants of the Lord to the remotest ages of time. Amen. "The day following, eight elders, viz., Joseph Smith, Jr., Oliver Cowdery, Sidney Rigdon, Peter Whitmer, Jr., Frederick G. Williams, Wm. W. Phelps, Martin Harris, and Joseph Coe, assembled together where the Temple is to be erected. Sidney Rigdon dedicated the ground where the city is to stand: and Joseph Smith, Jr., laid a stone at the northeast corner of the contemplated temple in the name of the Lord Jesus of Nazareth. After all present had rendered thanks to the great ruler of the universe, Sidney Rigdon pronounced this spot of ground wholly dedicated unto the Lord forever: Amen."

Some of the elders who traveled to the land of Missouri and preached by the way, tarried here in this land, among whom is the Bishop E. [Edward] Partridge, Isaac Morley and John Corrill. Some were sick on their way to the land, but all were restored to health. Among those who were sick were John Murdock, Parley P. Pratt and Thomas B. Marsh--They all tarried until after they attended a conference in this land. They have since all gone to preach the gospel and call sinners to repentance.

There were some Churches built by the way as they journeyed to this land (Missouri) and the people were warned of the danger they were in, if they did not repent.

And now when the elders had returned to their homes in Ohio, the churches needed much exhortation in the absence of the elders many apostatized: but many have returned again to the fold from whence they had strayed--And many mighty miracles were wrought by the elders--one in particular which I shall here notice--which was wrought by elders Emer Harris, Joseph Brackenberry and Wheeler Baldwin. Is an infirmity in an old lady who had been helpless for the space of eight years confined to her bed. She did not belong to this church, but sent her request to the elders--who immediately attended to her call, and after their arrival prayed for her, and laid their hands on her, and she was immediately made whole and magnified and praised God, and is now enjoying perfect health.

And thus the churches again prospered and the work of the Lord spread.

Shortly after Joseph Smith, Jr., Oliver Cowdery and Sidney Rigdon returned Sidney wrote a description and an epistle according to commandment. And Oliver Cowdery and Newel K. Whitney-- were commanded to go and visit the Churches speedily--as you will see by reading the revelation given August thirty at Kirtland--The following is a copy of the epistle written by [Sidney] Rigdon's own hand:

"I, Sidney, a servant of Jesus Christ by the will of God the Father and through the faith of our Lord Jesus Christ unto the Saints who are scattered abroad in the last days, may grace, mercy and peace, rest upon you from God the Father and from our Lord Jesus Christ, who is greatly to be feared, among his Saints and to be had in reverence of all them who obey him.

"Beloved Brethren,--

"It has pleased God even the Father to make known unto us in these last days, the good pleasure of his will concerning his Saints; and to make known unto us, the things which he has decreed upon the nations even wasting and destruction. Until they are utterly destroyed, and the earth made desolate by reason of the wickedness of its inhabitants according as he has made known in times past by the prophets and apostles, that such calamities should befall the inhabitants of the earth in the last days, unless they should repent and turn to the living God. And as the time is now near at hand, for the accomplishment of his purposes and the fulfillment of his prophecies, which have been spoken by all the holy prophets ever since the world began, he has sent and signified, unto us by the mouths of his holy prophets, that he has raised up in these last days--the speedy accomplishment of his purposes which shall be accomplished, on the heads of the rebellious of this generation-- among whom he has been pleased in much mercy and goodness to send forth the fullness of his gospel in order that they might repent and turn to the living God, and be made partakers of his Holy Spirit. But by reason of their wickedness and rebellion against him, and wicked and unbelieving hearts the Lord withdrew his spirit from them, and gives them up to work all uncleanliness with greediness, and to bring swift destruction on themselves--and through their wickedness to hasten the day of calamity, that they may be left without excuse in the day of vengeance.

"But it has pleased our Heavenly Father to make known some better things, concerning his Saints, and those who serve him in fear and rejoice in meekness before him, even things which pertain to life everlasting, for godliness has the promise of the life, that now is, and that which is to come; Even so it has pleased our Heavenly Father to make provisions for his Saints in these last days of tribulation that they through faith and patience, and by continuing in well-doing may preserve their lives; and attain unto rest and endless felicity--but by no other means, than that of a strict observance of his commandments and teachings in all things as there is and can be no ruler or lawgiver in the kingdom of God save it be God our Savior himself--and before him he requires that all his saints and those who have named the name of Jesus, should be careful to depart from iniquity--and serve him with fear, rejoicing and trembling, least he be angry and they perish from their way.

"According to the prediction of the ancient prophets that the Lord would send his messengers in the last days, and gather his elect (which is the elect according to the covenant, viz., those who like Abraham are faithful to God and the word of his grace) from the four winds even from one end of the earth to the other as testified of by the Savior himself--so in these last days, he has commenced to gather together, into a place provided before of God and had in reserve in days of old being kept by the power and providence of God, for this purpose and which he now holds in his own hands, that they through faith, and patience may inherit the promises--a land which God by his own commandment has consecrated to himself where he has said that his laws shall be kept, and where his saints can dwell in safety, through their perseverance in well-doing, and their unfeigned repentance of all their sins, our Heavenly Father has provided this land himself because it was the one which was the best adapted for his children, where Jew and Gentile might dwell together: for God has the same respect to all those who call upon him in truth and righteousness whether they be Jew and Gentile; for there is no respect of person with him.

"This land being situated in the center of the continent on which we dwell with an exceeding fertile soil and ready cleared for the hand of the cultivator bespeaks the goodness of our God, in providing so goodly a heritage, and its climate suited for persons from every quarter of this continent, either East, West, North and South. Yea I think I may say, for all constitutions from any portion the world, and its productions nearly all varieties of both grain and vegetables which are common in this country, together with all means, clothing: in addition to this it abounds with fountains of pure water, the soil climate at surface are all adapted, to health indeed I may say that the whole properties of the country invite the Saints to come, and partake of their blessings, but what more need I say about a country which our Heavenly Father holds in his hands, for if it were unhealthy he could make it healthy and if barren he could make it fruitful. Such is the land which the Lord has provided for us, in the last days for an inheritance, and truly it is a goodly land, and none other as well suited for all the Saints as this and all those who have faith and confidence in God who has ever seen this land will bear the same testimony. In order that you may understand the will of God respecting this land and the way and means of possessing it, I can only refer you to commandments which the Lord has delivered by the mouth of his prophets which will be read, to you, by our brethren Oliver Cowdery and Newel K. Whitney whom the Lord has appointed, to visit the Churches and obtain means for purchasing this our inheritance that we may escape in the day of tribulation which is coming on the earth. I conclude by exhorting you to hear the voice of the Lord your God who is speaking to you in much mercy and who is sending forth, his word and his revelation in these last days, in order that we may escape impending vengeance; and the judgments which await this generation, and which will speedily overtake them--brethren pray for me, that I may be counted worthy to obtain an inheritance in the land of Zion and to overcome, the World through faith, and dwell with the sanctified, forever, and ever Amen.

Written at Kirtland, Ohio August 31, 1831.

CHAPTER 10

Immediately after the commandment was given and the epistle written, Oliver Cowdery and N. [Newell] K. Whitney went from place to place and from Church to Church preaching and expounding the scriptures and commandments, and obtaining moneys of the disciples for the purpose of buying lands for the Saints according to commandments; and the disciples truly opened their hearts, and thus there have been lands purchased for the inheritance of the Saints.

Soon after this, the time of holding the General Conference drew near; and Joseph the Seer, and Sidney the Scribe, moved from Kirtland, Ohio, to Hiram, Portage County, and continued the translation of the New Testament.

On the twenty-fifth day of October, 1831, the elders assembled together at Irenus Burnett's in the township of Orange and county of Cuyahoga, Ohio. Twelve high priests; seventeen elders; five priests; and three teachers. At which conference were ordained one elder and fourteen priests, the names of whom you will find recorded in the conference minute book.

About this time it was in contemplation for Oliver Cowdery to go to Zion and carry with him the revelations and commandments; and I also received a revelation to go with him. We left Ohio on the 20th of November, 1831, and arrived in Zion, Missouri, January 5, 1832.

When we arrived at Zion we found the Saints in as good situation as we could reasonably expect.

January 23, 1832, held a conference in Zion, attended to the business of the Church, and licensed ten elders to go and preach the gospel.

In March, 1832, the enemies held a council in Independence, Jackson County, Missouri, how they might destroy the Saints; but did not succeed at this time. But continued their broils until they had expelled us from the city, as you will hereafter see.

There are at this time [March 1832] four hundred and two disciples living in this land Zion.

And it came to pass that Joseph the Seer and Sidney the Scribe, and N. [Newell] K. Whitney and one Jesse Gause came to Zion to comfort the Saints and settle some little difficulties, and regulate the Church and affairs concerning it. We had a pleasant visit with them and they returned again in peace. I will here mention one circumstance and the return of these brethren. While they were riding in a stagecoach, the horses ran away and upset the coach and broke N. K. Whitney's ankle bone. But notwithstanding, through the providence of God he soon got home; but is now somewhat infirm in consequence of aforesaid accident.

About these days the Lord gave a commandment for Joseph the Seer and N. K. Whitney, the bishop, at Kirtland, to go and cry repentance to the cities of Boston, New York, and Albany; and bear testimony of their utter abolishment if they did not repent and receive the gospel.

Zion is prospering at present and high priests are stationed to watch over the several branches.

December 1, 1832. There are now five hundred and thirty-eight individuals in this land belonging to the Church.

And it came to pass that in the fall of the year, 1832, the disciples at Ohio received the gift of tongues; and in June, 1833, we received the gift of tongues in Zion.

About these days we received the following epistle:

We, the undersigned citizens of Jackson County, believing that an important crisis is at hand, as regards our civil society, in consequence of a pretended religious sect of people that have settled and are still settling in our county, styling themselves Mormons, and intending to rid ourselves, peaceably if we can and forcibly if we must, and believing as we do, that the arm of civil law does not afford us a guarantee, or at least not a sufficient one against the evils which are now inflicted upon us, and seem to be increasing by the said religious sect, deem it expedient and of the highest importance to form ourselves into a company for the better and easier accomplishment of our purpose, which we deem almost superfluous to say is justified as well by the law of nature as by the law of self-preservation. It is more than two years since the first of these fanatics or knaves, (for one or the other they undoubtedly are), made their first appearance among us; and pretending as they did, and now do, to hold personal communion and converse face to face with the Most High God, to receive communications and revelations direct from heaven; to heal the sick by the laying on of hands; and in short, to perform all the wonder-working miracles wrought by the inspired apostles and prophets. We believed them deluded fanatics, or weak and designing knaves, and that they and their pretensions would soon pass away; but in this we were deceived.

The arts of a few designing leaders among them have thus far succeeded in holding them together as a society, and since the arrival of the first of them they have daily increased; and if they had been respectable citizens in society, and thus deluded, they would have been entitled to our pity rather than to our comtempt and hatred. But from their appearance; from their manners; and from their conduct, since their coming among us, we have every reason to believe that with but a very few exceptions, they were of the very dregs of that society from which they came; lazy, idle and vicious.

This we conceive is not idle assertion, but a fact susceptible of proof. For with these few exceptions above named, they brought into our county little or no property with them, and left less behind them, and we infer that those only yoked themselves to the Mormon car who had nothing earthly or heavenly to lose by the change; and we fear that if some of the leaders among them had paid the forfeit due to crime instead of being chosen ambassadors of the Most High, they would have been inmates of solitary cells. But their conduct here stamps their characters in their true color. More than a year it has been ascertained that they have been tampering with our slaves, and endeavoring to sow dissension and raise sedition among them. Of this their Mormon leaders were informed, and they said they would deal with any of their members who should again in like case offend. But how spurious are appearances. In a late number of the Star printed in Independence by the leaders of the sect, there is an article inviting free negroes and mulattoes from other states to become Mormons and move and settle among us. This exhibits them in still more odious colors. It manifests a desire on the part of their society to inflict on our society an injury that they know would be to us entirely unsupportable, and one of the surest means of driving us from the country; for it would require none of the supernatural gifts that they pretend to, to see that the introduction of such a cast among us would corrupt our blacks and instigate them to bloodshed.

They openly blaspheme the Most High God and cast comtempt on his holy religion by pretending to receive revelations direct from heaven; by pretending to speak in unknown tongues by direct inspiration, and by divine pretentions derogatory of God and religion, and to the utter subversion of human reason.

They declare openly that God has given them this county of land; and that sooner or later they must and will have possession of our lands for an inheritance; and in fine, they have conducted themselves on many other occasions in such a manner that we believe it a duty we owe ourselves, to our wives and children, to the cause of public morals, to remove them from among us as we are not prepared to give up our possessions to them, or to receive into the bosom of our families as fit companions for our wives and daughters the degraded and corrupted free negroes and mulattoes that are now invited to settle among us.

Under such a state of things even our beautiful country would cease to be a desirable residence, and our situation intolerable.

We therefore agree that after timely warning, and upon receiving an adequate compensation for what little property they cannot take with them, they refuse to leave us in peace as they found us, we agree to use such means as will be sufficient to remove them; and to that end we pledge to each other our bodily powers, our lives, fortunes, and sacred honor.

We will meet at the court-house in the town of Independence on Saturday next, 20th inst., to consult of ulterior movements.

July 15, 1833

A committee was appointed at the foregoing meeting, and waited on us, Partridge, Corrill, Phelps, etc. The committee consisted of Lewis Franklin, Mr. Campbell, Judge Lucas, Judge Fristoe, Russel Hicks, Mr. Simpson, two of the Mr. Wilsons, Captain Tipits, and Mr. Cummings.

To answer them this question, "Will you leave this county or not?" Allowing us only fifteen minutes to answer the question. We did not make any reply at that time.

The committee further required of us to shut up our printing-office, store, mechanical shops, etc., immediately, and leave the county.

Those who waited on the committee were A. S. Gilbert, Edward Partridge, Isaac Morley, John Corrill, W.[William] W. Phelps, and John Whitmer.

When they found that we were unwilling to comply with their requests they returned to the court-house and voted to raze the printing to the ground, which they immediately did; and at the same time took Edward Partridge and Charles Allen and tarred and feathered them, threatening to kill us if we did not leave the county immediately.

They were also determined to demolish the store. A. S. Gilbert prevailed on them to let it stand until Tuesday next, and have time to pack his goods himself.

Tuesday arrived and death and destruction stared us in the face. The whole county turned out and surrounded us; came to W.[William] W. Phelps' and my house and took us upon the public square, as also Partridge, Corrill, Morley, and Gilbert, and were determined to massacre us unless we agreed to leave the county immediately. Finally we agreed to leave upon the following condition:

July 23, 1833. It is understood that the undersigned members of the said society do give their solemn pledge each for himself as follows: That Oliver Cowdery, W. W. Phelps, William E. McLellin, Edward Partridge, Lyman Wight, Simeon Carter, Peter and John Whitmer, and Harvey Whitlock shall remove with their families out of this county on or before the first day of January next; and that they as well as the two hereinafter named, use all their influence to induce all the brethren now here to move as soon as possible, one body say by the first of January next, and all by the first day of April next, and to advise and try all means in their power, to stop any more of their sect from moving to this county. As to those now on the road, and who have notice of this agreement, they will use their influence to prevent their settling permanently in the county, but that they shall only make arrangements for temporary shelter till a new location is fixed on by the society. John Corrill and A. S. Gilbert are allowed to remain as general agents to wind up the business of the society so long as necessity shall require; and said Gilbert may sell out his goods now on hand, but is to make no new importation. The Star is not again to be published nor a press set up by the society in this county. If the said E. Partridge and W. W. Phelps move their families by the first of January as aforesaid, that they themselves will be allowed to go and come in order to transact and wind up their business. The committee pledge themselves to use all their influence to prevent any violence being used so long as a compliance with the foregoing terms is observed by the parties concerned.

Signed, Samuel C. Owens, Llonidas Oldham, G. W. Simpson, W. L. Irvin, John Harris, Henry Childs, Harry H. Younger, Hugh L. Brazeale, N. K. Olmstead, William Bowers, Z. Waller, Harman Gregg, Aaron Overton, Samuel Weston.

The battle was fought on the evening of the fourth day of November, and only one of the brethren was killed, and two of the mob. David Whitmer headed the disciples.

INDEPENDENCE, October 30, 1833.

About these days we employed counselors to assist in prosecuting the law, which we had been advised by J. Smith, Junior, the Seer, to do. They employed Doniphan, Atchison, Rees, and Wood, of Liberty, Clay County, Missouri, who engaged to carry on our suits for $1,000, which was agreed to be paid by E. Partridge and W. W. Phelps, which came from the Church.

The Church was driven by the mob of Jackson County on the 4th of November, 1833; and on the night of the 13th of the same month the stars fell.

CHAPTER 11

The situation of our brethren after leaving their homes in Jackson in the most distressing circumstances, in the cold month of November, found it difficult to preserve life in many instances. Some fled with but few clothes, leaving their beds and bedding; others taking with them what they could carry and running for their lives; women losing some of their children while fleeing for their lives; and thus you may judge how the poor Saints have suffered, after having given only a few hints of the distress.

You will find in one of the numbers of the Star, printed at Kirtland, Ohio, a piece headed "The Mormons," which will serve to illustrate, dated February, 1834.

I would here remark that a full account of the proceedings of the Jackson mob is published in the Star at Kirtland, commencing at No. 15 to the end of the volume.

LIBERTY, Clay County, February 19, 1834.
To the Judge, John F. Ryland, of the Fifth Circuit of Missouri

Sir: Learning that a court of inquiry is to be held in Jackson County at the next regular term of the Circuit Court for the county; or that some kind of legal proceedings is to commence for the purpose of obtaining the facts, as far as can be, to the criminal transactions and riotous proceedings, or bringing to punishment the guilty in that county.

We therefore pray your honor to avail yourself of every means in your power to execute the law and make it honorable, and believing that the testimony of some of the members of our Church will be important, and deeming it unsafe to risk our persons in that county without a guard, we request that the order from the executive already transmitted may be put in force.

Respectfully,

EDWARD PARTRIDGE. W. W. PHELPS. JOHN WHITMER. A. S. GILBERT. JOHN CORRILL.

Clay County, April 9, 1834. (This date is given by Joseph Smith as April 10.--H. C. S.)

Dear Sir: Notwithstanding you may have become tired of receiving communications from us, yet we beg leave of your Excellency to pardon us of this as we have this week enclosed a petition to the President of the United States, (A. Jackson,) setting forth our distressed condition, together with your excellency's views of it, as well as the limited powers with which you are clothed to afford that protection which we need to enjoy our rights and la in Jackson County. A few lines from the governor of this state, in connection with our humble entreaties for our possessions and privileges, we think would be of considerable consequence towards bringing about the desired object, and would be gratefully acknowledged by us, and our society, and we may add, by all honorable men.

We therefore, as humble petitioners, ask the favor of your excellency to write to the President (A. Jackson) of the United States of America, that he may assist us, or our society in obtaining our rights in Jackson County, and help protect us when there till we are safe; and in duty bound we will pray.

W. W. PHELPS. E. PARTRIDGE. J. WHITMER. JOHN CORRILL. A. S. GILBERT.

DANIEL DUNKLIN, Governor of Missouri.

LIBERTY, CLAY COUNTY, MISSOURI, April 10, 1834.

To the President of the United States of America:

We, the undersigned, your humble petitioners, citizens of the United States of America, being members of the Church of Christ reproachfully called Mormons, beg leave to refer the President to our former petition, dated October last, and also to lay before him the accompanying handbill, dated December 12, 1833, with assurance that the said handbill exhibits but a faint sketch of the suffering of your petitioners and their brethren up to the period of its publication.

The said handbill shows that at the time of dispersion part of our families fled into the new and unsettled county of Van Buren. Being unable to procure provisions in that county through the winter, many of them were compelled to return to their homes in Jackson County or perish with hunger. But they had no sooner set foot upon that soil, which a few months before we had purchased of the United States, than they were again met by the citizens of Jackson County and a renewal of savage barbarity inflicted upon them by beating with clubs and sticks, presenting knives and firearms, and threatening with death if they did not immediately flee from the county. The inhuman assaults upon these families were repeated two or three times through the last winter, till they were compelled at last to leave their possessions in Jackson County and flee with their mangled bodies into this county (Clay), here to mingle their tears and unite their supplications with hundreds of their brethren to our Heavenly Father and the chief ruler of our nation.

Between one and two thousand of the people called Mormons, have been driven by the force of arms from the county of Jackson, in this state, since the first of November last, being compelled to leave their highly cultivated fields, the greater part of which had been bought of the United States, and of all this of our belief in direct revelation from God to the children of men, according to the Holy Scriptures. We know that such illegal violence s not been inflicted upon any sect or community of people by the citizens of the United States since the Declaration of Independence.

That this is a religious persecution is notorious throughout our country. When accomplices in these unparalleled outrages, engaged in the destruction of the printing-office, dwelling-house, etc.; yet the records of the judicial tribunals of that county are not stained by a crime by our people. Our numbers being greatly inferior to the enemy, we were unable to stand in self-defense. And our lives at this day are continually threatened by that infuriated people, so that our personal safety forbids one of our members going into that county on business. We beg leave to state that no impartial investigation into this criminal matter can be made, because the offenders must be tried in the county in which the offense was committed, and the inhabitants of the county, both magistrates and people, being combined, with the exception of a few, justice cannot be expected. At this day your petitioners do not know of a solitary family belonging to our Church but what have been violently expelled from Jackson County by the inhabitants thereof. Your petitioners have not gone into detail with an account of their individual sufferings, from death and bruised bodies and the universal distress which prevails at this day in a greater or less degree, throughout our whole body, not only because those sacred rights are guaranteed to every religious sect have been publicly invaded in open hostility to the spirit and genius of our free government, but such of their houses as have not been burned their beds and most of their products of the labor of their hands for the last year have been wrested from them by a band of outlaws, congregated in Jackson County, on the western boundaries of the state of Missouri, within about thirty miles of the United States military post, at Fort Leavenworth on the Missouri River. Your petitioners say that they do not enter into a minute detail of their sufferings in this petition least they should weary the patience of their venerable chief, whose arduous duties they know are great, and daily accumulating.

We only hope to show to him that this is an unprecedented emergency in the history of our country--that the magistracy thereof is set at defiance, and justice checked in the open violation of its laws; and that we your petitioners, who are almost wholly native born citizens of these United States of America, of whom they purchased their land in Jackson County, Missouri, with intent to cultivate the same, as peaceable citizens, are now forced from them, and dwelling in the counties of Clay, Ray, and Lafayette, in the state of Missouri, without permanent homes, and suffering all the privations which must necessarily result from such inhuman treatment. Under these sufferings your petitioners petitioned the Governor of this state in December last, in answer to which they received the following letter:

"City of Jefferson, February 4, 1834.

Your communication of the 6th of December was regularly received and duly considered; and had I not expected to receive the evidence brought out on the inquiry ordered into the military conduct of Colonel Pitcher in a short time after I received your petition I should have replied long since.

Last evening I was informed that the further inquiry of the court was postponed until the 20th inst. Then before I can have anything from this court the court of civil jurisdiction will hold its session in Jackson County, consequently cannot receive anything from one preparatory to arragement from the other.

I am very sensible indeed of the injury your people complain of, and should consider myself very remiss in the discharge of my duties even were I not to do everything in my power consistent with the legal exercise of them, to afford your society redress to which they seem entitled. One of your requests needs no evidence to support the right to have it granted, it is that your people be put in possession of their homes from which they have been expelled. But what may be the duties of the executive after that, will depend upon contingencies. If upon inquiry it is found your people were wrongfully dispossessed of their arms of Colonel Pitcher, then an order will be issued to have them returned; and should your men organize according to law, which they have a right to do, (indeed it is their duty to do so unless exempted by religious scruples,) and apply for public arms, the executive could not distinguish between their rights to have them and the right of any other description of people similarly situated.

As the request for keeping up a military force to protect your people and prevent the commission of crimes, were I to comply it would transcend the powers with which the executive of this state is clothed.

The Federal Constitution has given to Congress the power to provide for calling forth the militia to execute the laws of the Union, suppress insurrections or repel invasions; and for these purposes the President of the United States is authorized to make the call upon the executive of the respective states. And the laws of the state empower 'the commander-in-chief in case of actual or threatened invasion, insurrection or war, or public danger, or other emergency, to call forth into actual service such portions of the militia as he may deem expedient.' These together with the general provisions in our state constitution that 'The Governor shall take care that the laws are faithfully executed,' and call upon his branch of executive power. None of these as I consider embrace this part of your request.

The 'Words, or other emergencies,' in our militia law, seem quite broad, but the emergency to come within the object of that provision should be of a public nature. Your case is certainly a very emergent one, and the consequences as important to your society as if the war had been waged against the whole state; yet the public has no other interest in it than that the laws be faithfully executed. This far, I presume the whole community feel a deep interest, for that which is the case of the Mormons of today, may be the case of the Catholics tomorrow, and after them any other sect that may become obnoxious to a majority of the people of any section of the state. So far as a faithful execution of the laws are concerned, the executive is disposed to do everything consistent with the means furnished him by the legislature, and I think I may safely say the same of the judiciary.

As now advised I am of opinion that a military guard will be necessary to protect the state witnesses and officers of the court, and to assist in the execution of its orders while sitting in Jackson County. By this mail I write to Mr. Reese enclosing him an order on the captain of the 'Liberty Blues,' requiring the captain to comply with the requisition of the Circuit Attorney in protecting the court and officers, and executing their precepts and orders, during the process of the trials. Under the protection of this guard, your people can if they think proper, return to their homes in Jackson County, and be protected in them during the progress of the trials in question, by which time facts will be developed upon which I can act more definitely. The attorney-general will be required to assist the circuit attorney if they latter deems it necessary.

On the subject of civil injuries I must refer you to the courts; such questions rest with them exclusively. The laws are sufficient to afford a remedy for every injury of this kind; and whenever you make out a case entitling you to damages there can be no doubt entertained of their ample reward.

Justice is sometimes slow in its progress, but it is not less sure on this account.

(Signed) Very Respectfully Your Obedient Servant,
DANIEL DUNKLIN."

"TO MESSRS. W. W. PHELPS, ISAAC MORLEY, JOHN WHITMER, EDWARD PARTRIDGE, JOHN CORRILL, and A. S. GILBERT."

By the foregoing letter from the Governor, the President will perceive a disposition manifested by him to enforce the laws as far as means have been furnished by the legislature of this state. But the powers vested in the executive of this state seem to be inadequate for relieving the distresses of your petitioners in this present emergency. He is willing to send a guard to conduct our families back to their possessions, but it not authorized to direct a military force to be stationed any length of time for the protection of your petitioners. This step would be laying (the foundation for) a more fatal tragedy than the first, as our numbers at present are too small to contend single-handed with the mob of said county; and as the Federal Constitution has given to Congress the power to provide for calling forth the militia to execute the laws of the Union, suppress insurrections, or repel invasions; "And for these purposes the President of the United States is authorized to make the call upon the executives of the respective states." Therefore we your petitioners in behalf of our society, which is so scattered and suffering, most humbly pray that we may be restored to our lands, homes, and property in Jackson County, and protected in them by an armed force till peace can be restored, and as in duty bound we will ever pray.

Signed by 51 leading members of the said Church.

LIBERTY, CLAY COUNTY, MISSOURI, April 10, 1834.

To the President of the United States of America:

We, the undersigned, whose names are subscribed to the accompanying petition, some of the leading members of The Church of Christ, beg leave to refer the President to the handbill and petition herewith. We are not insensible of the multiplicity of business and numerous petitions, by which care and perplexity of our chief ruler is daily increased; and it is with diffidence that we venture to lay before the executive at this emergent period these two documents, wherein is briefly portrayed, the most unparalleled persecution and flagrant outrage of law that has disgraced our country since the Declaration of Independence. But knowing the independent fortitude and vigorous energy for preserving the rights of the citizens of this republic which has hitherto marked course of our chief magistrate, we are encouraged to hope, that this communication will not pass unnoticed; but that the President will consider our locations on the extreme frontier of the United States, exposed to many ignorant and lawless ruffians, who are already congregated and determined to nullify all law that will procure to your petitioners the privilege of a peaceable possession of their lands in Jackson County.

We again repeat, that our society is wandering in adjoining counties at this day, bereft of their houses and lands, and threatened with death by the aforesaid outlaws of Jackson County. And lest the President should be deceived in regard to our true situation, by the misrepresentation of certain individuals, who are disposed to cover the gross outrages of the mob, from religious, political, and speculative motives, we beg leave to refer him to the Governor of Missouri, at the same time informing him that the number of men composing the mob of Jackson County may be estimated at from three to five hundred, most of them prepared with firearms.

After noting the statements here made if it should be the disposition of the President to grant aid, we must humbly entreat that early relief may be extended to suffering families, who are now expelled from their possessions by firearms. Our lands in Jackson County are about thirty miles distant from Fort Leavenworth, on the Missouri River.

With due respect we are, Sir, Your Obedient Servants,

A. S. Gilbert. W. W. Phelps. Edward Partridge. John Whitmer. John Corrill.

P. S.--In February last a number of our people were marched under a guard furnished by the governor of the state into Jackson County for the purpose of prosecuting the mob criminally; but the attorney-general of the state, and the district attorney, knowing the force and power of the mob, advised us to relinquish all hopes of criminal prosecution to effect anything against the band of outlaws, and we returned under guard without the least prospect of our obtaining our rights and possessions in Jackson County with any other means than a few companies of the United States regular troops to guard and assist us until we are safely settled.

Signed by the same as the foregoing.

LIBERTY, Clay County, Missouri, April 24, 1834.

Dear Sir: In your last communication of the 9th inst., we omitted to make inquiry concerning the evidence brought out before the court of inquiry in the case of Colonel Pitcher. The court met pursuant to adjournment on 20th of February last and for some reason unknown to us we have not been able to ascertain information concerning the opinion or decision of the court. We had hoped that the testimony would have been transmitted to your Excellency before this, that an order might be issued for the return of our arms, of which we have been wrongfully dispossessed, as we believe will clearly appear to the Commander-in-Chief when the evidence is laid before him. As suggested in your communication of February 4, we had concluded to organize according to law and apply for public arms but we feared that such a step which must be attended with public ceremonies, might produce some excitement. We have thus far delayed any movement of that nature, hoping to regain our arms from Jackson County that we might independently equip ourselves and be prepared to assist in the maintenance of our constitutional rights and liberties as guaranteed to us by our country, and also to defend our persons and property from a lawless mob, when it shall please the executive, at some future day, to put us in possession of our homes, from which we have been most wickedly expelled.

We are happy to make an expression of thanks for the willingness manifested by the executive to enforce the laws as far as he can constitutionally, "with the means furnished him by the Legislature;" and we are firmly persuaded that a future day will verify to him, that whatever aid we receive from the executive, has not been lavished upon a band of traitors, but upon a people whose respect and veneration for the laws of our country, and its pure republican principles are as great as that of any other society in the United States.

As our Jackson foes and their correspondents are busy in circulating slanderous and wicked reports concerning our people, their views, etc., we have deemed it expedient to inform your Excellency that we have received communications from our (friends) at the East informing us that a number of brethren, perhaps two or three hundred, would come to Jackson County in the course of the ensuing season; and we are satisfied that when the Jackson mob get the intelligence that a large number of our people are about to remove into that county, they will raise a great hue and cry, and circulate many bugbears through the medium of their favorite press. But we think your Excellency is well aware that our object is purely to defend ourselves and possessions against another unparalleled attack from that mob, inasmuch as the executive of this state cannot keep a military force "to protect our people in that county without transcending his powers." We want therefore the privilege of defending ourselves, and the Constitution of our country while God is willing we should have a being on his footstool.

We do not know at what (time) our friends from the East will arrive; but expect more certain intelligence in a few weeks. Whenever they do arrive it would be the wish of our people in this county, to return to our homes in company with our friends, under guard, and when once more in legal possession of our homes in

Jackson County we will endeavor to take care of them without further wearying the patience of our worthy chief magistrate. We will write hereafter or send an express--during the intermediate time we would be glad to hear of the prospect of securing our arms.

With due respect, we are Sir, Your Obedient Servants,

A. S. GILBERT. W. W. PHELPS. E. PARTRIDGE. JOHN CORRILL. JOHN WHITMER.

CHAPTER 12

I will here remark that the Saints are and were preparing to go back to Jackson County as soon as the way should open. We had hard struggling to obtain a living, as may well be understood, being driven, having no money or means to subsist upon, and being among strangers in a strange place; being despised, mocked at, and laughed to scorn by some, and pitied by others; thus we lived from November, 1833, till May 1834, and but little prospect yet to return to our homes in Jackson County in safety--the mob rages and the people's hearts are hardened, and the Saints are few in number, and poor, afflicted, cast out, and smitten by their enemies.

I will further state, because of the scattered situation and the many perplexities, I am not in possession of all the letters and information that I wish I was, and some that are in my possession are not arranged according to date because of the situation I am in, being poor, and write as I can obtain intelligence, and find time between sun and sun to write.

CITY OF JEFFERSON, April 20, 1834.
To Messrs. Phelps, Partridge, Corrill, Whitmer, and Gilbert:
Gentlemen: Yours of the ninth inst. was received yesterday, in which you request me, as executive of this state, to join you in an appeal to the President of the United States for protection in the enjoyment of your rights in Jackson County. It will readily occur to you no doubt, the possibility of having asked of the President in a way that he no more than the executive of this state could render. If you have petitioned for that which I would be of opinion he has power to grant I should have no objection to join in urging it upon him; but I could no more ask the President, however willing I am to see your society restored to and protected in their rights, to do that which I think he has no power to do, than I would do such an act

myself. If you will send me a copy of your petition to the President, I will judge of his right to grant it; and if of the opinion he possesses the power I will write in favor of its exercise.

I am now in correspondence with the Federal Government, on the subject of deposits of munitions of war, on our Northern and Western boundaries, and have no doubt but shall succeed in procuring one, which (will) be located if left to me, (and the Secretary of War seems to be willing to be governed by the opinion of the Executive of the state,) somewhere near the state line either in Jackson or Clay County.

The establishment will be an (arsenal), and will probably be under the command of a lieutenant of the army. This will afford you the best means of military protection the nature of your case will admit.

Although I can see no direct impropriety in making the subject of this paragraph public, yet I should prefer it not to be so considered, for the present, as the erection of an arsenal is only in expectancy.

Permit me to suggest to you, that as you have now greatly the advantage over your enemies, in public estimation, that there is a great propriety in retaining that advantage, which you can easily do by keeping your adversaries in the wrong. The law both civil and military seems to be deficient in affording your society proper protection; nevertheless public sentiment is a powerful corrective of error, and you should make it your policy to continue to deserve it.

With much respect and great regard I am Your Obedient Servant,

DANIEL DUNKLIN.

CITY OF JEFFERSON, May 2, 1834.
TO MESSRS. W. W. PHELPS AND OTHERS.

Gentlemen: Yours of the 24th ult. is before me; in reply to which can inform you that becoming impatient at delay of the court of enquiry in making their report in the case of Lieutenant Colonel Pitcher, on the 11th ult. I wrote to General Thompson for the reason of such delay. Last night I received his reply, and with it the report of the court of enquiry, from the tenor of which I find no difficulty in deciding that the arms your people were required to surrender on the fifth of November should be returned; and have issued an order to Colonel Lucas to deliver them to you or to your order, which order is here enclosed.

Respectfully Your Obedient Servant,
(Signed) DANIEL DUNKLIN.

CITY OF JEFFERSON, May 2, 1834.
TO S. D. LUCAS, Colonel 33 Regiment.

Sir: The court ordered to enquire into the conduct of Lieutenant Colonel Pitcher in the movement he made on the 5th November last, report it as their unanimous opinion that there was no insurrection on that day; and that Lieutenant Colonel Pitcher was not authorized to call out his troops on the 5th November, 1833. It was unnecessary to require the Mormons to give up their arms. Therefore you will deliver to W. W. Phelps, Edward Partridge, John Corrill, John Whitmer and A. S. Gilbert or their order, the fifty-two guns and one pistol reported by Lieutenant Colonel Pitcher to you on the 5th December last, as having been received by him from the Mormons on the 5th of the preceding October.

Respectfully,
DANIEL DUNKLIN, Commander in Chief.
Liberty County, May 7, 1834.

Dear Sir: Your favor of the 20th ult. came to hand the first inst. which gives us a gleam of hope that the time will come when we may experience a partial mitigation of our sufferings. The salutary advice in the conclusion of your letter is received with great deference.

Since our last of the 24th ult. the mob of Jackson County have burned our dwellings. As near as we can ascertain between 100 and 150 were consumed by fire in about one week. Our arms were also taken from the depository (the jail) about ten days since, and distributed among the mob. Great efforts are now making by the mob to stir up the citizens of this county, and Lafayette to commit similar outrages against us; but we think they will fail in accomplishing their wicked designs in this county.

We here annex a copy of the petition to the president.

With Great Respect, Your Obedient Servants,

A. S. GILBERT. W. W. PHELPS.

COLONEL S. D. LUCAS. LIBERTY, May 15, 1834.

Sir: We have this day received a communication from the governor of this state covering the order herewith, and we hasten to forward the said order to you by the bearer Mr. Richardson, who is instructed to receive your reply.

We would further remark that under existing circumstances we hope to receive our arms on this side the river, and we would name a place near one of the ferries for your convenience. As the arms are few in number, we request that they may be delivered as soon as possible.

Respectfully yours,

A. S. GILBERT, W. W. PHELPS, J. CORRILL, E. PARTRIDGE, JOHN WHITMER.

CHAPTER 13

June 1, 1834.

The Jackson County mob have sent a Mr. Samuel Campbell to harangue the people of Clay County on the subject of mobocracy. For they anticipated that they needed help, therefore they sent runners in the adjoining counties to strengthen themselves against the day when the camp should arrive. I mean the company headed by Joseph Smith, Jr., the seer, who were now on their way to this land. Campbell succeeded in embittering the minds of some, and the idea that Joseph should venture to bring an armed force into this upper country to afford relief to the poor and afflicted Saints, enraged the enemy, and darkness, gloom, and consternation pervaded the countenance of every enemy that was seen in this upper country. Some said they were fearful of the consequences of such a bold attempt; others were fearful of their lives and fortunes, and thus it was.

The aforesaid Campbell had a petition to get signers to turn at and help them. He went from place to place and held meetings for that purpose, but obtained only about twenty signers in Clay County.

The Saints here are preparing with all possible speed to arm themselves and otherwise prepare to go to Jackson County, when the camp arrives; for we have had some hints from Joseph the Seer, that this will be our privilege; so we were in hopes that the long wished-for day will soon arrive, and Zion be redeemed to the joy and satisfaction of the poor suffering Saints.

The mob of Jackson County proposed to sell us, or buy our possessions in a manner that they knew that we could not comply with if we were ever so willing, which served to blind the mind of those who had heretofore said nothing, but now advised us to comply because they thought we had better have something than nothing for our possessions.

The camp now arrived at Fishing River, where the enemy desired to head them, being led by priests, etc. But God interposed, and sent a storm of thunder, lightening, and rain at an astonishing rate, which stopped our enemies in consequence of the flood of water which swelled the river and made it impossible.

Joseph the Seer had frequently exhorted the Saints on their way up that if they would not heed his words the Lord would scourge them. The cholera broke out in the camp and several died with it to the grief and sorrow of the brethren and lamentation of their wives and families. The camp immediately scattered in the counties of Ray and Clay. Some returned immediately while others tarried. Received a revelation that it was not wisdom to go to Jackson County at this time, and that the armies of Israel should become very great and terrible first, and the servants of the Lord (shall have) been endowed with power from on high previous to the redemption of Zion.

Thus our fond hopes of being redeemed at this time were blasted at least for a season.

The first elders were to receive their endowment at Kirtland, Ohio, in the House of the Lord, built in that stake.

CHAPTER 14

Joseph the Seer began to set in order the Church in this country. Commenced to organize a high council according to the pattern received in Kirtland, Ohio. After which Joseph Smith, Jr., F. G. Williams and others returned to Kirtland, and the Saints remained in their places of abode to wait the due time of the Lord to be redeemed from wicked mobbers.

We, the inhabitants of Zion, wrote an appeal signed by W. W. Phelps, David Whitmer, John Whitmer, E. Partridge, John Corrill, I. Morley, P. P. Pratt, Lyman Wight, Newel Knight, T. B. Marsh, Simeon Carter, and Calvin Beebe, Missouri, July, 1834, and published at Kirtland in an extra Star, August 1834. ill

The above appeal and the following petition was accompanied. The petition reads as follows:

TO HIS EXCELLENCY, DANIEL DUNKLIN, governor of the state of Missouri:

The undersigned respectfully show that a large number of the citizens of the United States, inhabitants of the state of Missouri, professing to be The Church of Latter Day Saints, wrongfully called Mormons, having been illegally and cruelly driven from their lands and homes in Jackson County, Missouri, by a lawless mob (as your Excellency has already been informed) should by some ample means be restored to their possessions and rights; but as the said mob of Jackson County has considerably spread itself, and organized into an independent branch of government, by appointing a "Commander-in-Chief," and by preparing to resist the said Church even to blood-shed and that, too, with not only the common weapons used for self-defense and military discipline, but with cannon. Therefore your petitioners humbly ask your Excellency while the said Church is preparing to return, to petition the President of the United States for a guard of troops to be stationed in Jackson County sufficient to protect this unfortunate people in their rights as well as imposing enough to quell the Jackson County mob, for the honor of the state of Missouri.

In asking this favor of the governor while such great mob as that of July last in the city of New York, and others in other states, have been promptly put down by military or other exertion, your petitioners feel confident, that he will use all honorable means to restore this suffering body of citizens to all their constitutional rights and enjoyments, for the good of society and the safety of freemen, at the same sparing no pains to bring mobbers to justice, and crush mobbing in a country which professes to be governed by wholesome laws; and your petitioners will ever pray.

While all the foregoing letters and petitions were circulating, the Saints were humbling themselves before the Lord. But some were making preparation to leave the land, others were doubting the truth of the Book of Mormon, others denying the faith, others growing in grace and in the knowledge of the truth.

April 28, 1835

This day myself and family in company with W. W. Phelps and his son Waterman, started for Kirtland, Ohio, in obedience to the direction of Joseph the Seer.

Pretty much all the first elders had left for Kirtland previous to our going; some went on a tour preaching in their several courses.

While we were in trouble in Missouri the Saints in Kirtland, Ohio, had trouble also; but God had decreed to keep a strong-hold in Kirtland for five years, therefore, the wicked did not prevail, and the house of the Lord was building and the Saints gathering and preparing for the great day when the Lord should condescend to endow his first elders according to his promises, that his work might roll forth and be established according to his decree in the last days, that he might gather together his elect from the four quarters of the earth and be prepared when the veil of the covering of all flesh shall be taken off or away, and Zion become the joy of all the earth.

Arrived at Kirtland the 17th of May. Found the brethren in good health and spirits and prospering. The House of the Lord was raised and the stone-work thereof completed; the rafters were just put up and the first story of the steeple raised.

CHAPTER 15

KIRTLAND, OHIO, May 26, 1835.

Soon after our arrival in this place we held many councils, and one in particular I will here notice in which were several selections made, for particular individuals, according to the direction of the Spirit of the Lord through Joseph the Revelator, for inheritances in Zion as follows, first: Martin Harris 1, J. Smith, Jr., 2, Oliver Cowdery 3, David Whitmer 4, Sidney Rigdon 5, Edward Partridge 6, I. Morley 7, John Corrill 8, N. K. Whitney 9, Reynolds Cahoon 10, Hiram [Hyrum] Smith 11, J. Smith Sr., 12, Peter Whitmer 13, John Whitmer 14, F. G. Williams 15, W. W. Phelps 16, S. H. Smith 17, Wm. Smith 18, D. C. Smith 19, Christian Whitmer 20, Jacob Whitmer 21, Peter Whitmer, Jr., 22, Joseph Knight 23, Newel Knight 24, Joseph Knight, Jr., 25, Hezekiah Peck 26, Ezekiel Peck 27, Philo Dibble 28, Calvin Beebe 29, Isaiah Baker 30, Titus Billings 31, T. B. Marsh 32, Hiram Page 33, Simeon Carter 34, Jared Carter 35, Solomon Daniels 36, J. M. Burk 37, P. P. Pratt 38, Orson Pratt 39, John Murdock 40, John Johnson 41, Luke Johnson 42, Lyman E. Johnson 43, Orson Hyde 44, Joshua Lewis 45, Solomon Hancock 46, Levi Hancock 47, Zebedee Coltun [Coltrin] 48, Lyman Wight 49, Joseph Coe 50, Daniel Stanton 51, Freeborn Demill 52, Lewis Abbott 53, Jesse Hitchcock 54, John Smith 55, Adolphus Chapin 56, Able Pryor 57, George Pitkin 58, Truman Brace 59, Edmund Durfee 60, Brigham Young 61, A. C. Graves 62, David Pettigrew 63.

Some time in May the Twelve Apostles were chosen and ordained according to revelation given to D. [David] Whitmer and Oliver Cowdery.

The following are the names of the Twelve:

T. B. Marsh, D. W. Patton, P. P. Pratt, Orson Hyde, H. C. Kimball, Orson Pratt, Luke Johnson, L. E. Johnson, Brigham Young, W. E. McLellin, J. F. Boynton, William B. Smith.

On the morning of the 5th of May the Twelve took leave of their families and brethren, to fill their first mission under this commission, being commissioned to carry the gospel to Gentile and also unto Jew, having the keys of the gospel to unlock and then call on others to promulgate the same.

About the same time there were 70 high priests chosen, who were called elders, to be under the direction of the Twelve and assist them according to their needs; and if 70 were not enough, call 70 more until 70 times 70.

Out of the first seventy were selected, chosen, and ordained, for presidents, 7, namely: Zebedee Coltun [Coltrin] 1, Sylvester Smith 2, Leonard Rich 3, Hazen Aldrich 4, Joseph Young 5, Lyman Sherman 6, Levi Hancock 7.

The charge given by Oliver Cowdrey, David Whitmer, and Martin Harris, together with their blessings you will find recorded in the history kept by the Twelve and also by the Seventies.

CHAPTER 16

In June, 1835, a man by the name of Hewet came from England, and presented to a council the following letter as follows:

Dear Brethren in the Lord: At a council of the pastors of our Church held March 28, 1835, upon the propriety of the Reverend John Hewet visiting you, it was resolved and approved, that as he had an anxious desire to go to America, to see the things spoken of in one of your papers, brought here by a merchant from New York, he should have as he desired the sanction of the council, and if it pleased the Lord his approval.

The Lord has seen our joy and gladness to hear that he was raising up a people, for himself in that part of the new world as well as here. Oh may our faith increase that we may have evangelists, apostles and prophets, filled with the power of the Spirit, and performing his will in destroying the work of darkness.

The Reverend, Mr. Hewet, was professor of mathematics in Rotherdam Independent Seminary, and four years pastor in Barnsley Independent Church. He commenced preaching the doctrine we taught about two years since, and was excommunicated, many of his flock followed him so that eventually he was installed in the same church, and the Lord's work prospered. As he is a living epistle you will have if all be well, a full explanation. Many will follow should he approve of the country, etc.; who will help the cause because the Lord has favored them with this world's goods.

We had an utterance during our meeting which caused us to sing for joy. The Lord was pleased with our brother's holy determination to see you, and we understand that persecution had been great among you or would be; but we were commanded not to fear for he would be with us. Praise the Lord! The time is at hand when distance shall be no barrier between us, but when on the wings of love Jehovah's messengers shall be communicated by his Saints.

The Lord bless our brother, and may he prove a blessing to you. Be not afraid of our enemies, they shall unless they repent, be cast down by the Lord of Hosts. The workers of iniquity have been used by the Prince of Darkness, to play the counterfeit, but discernment has been given, that they were immediately put to shame by being detected, so that the flock never suffered as yet by them. Grace, mercy and peace be with you from God our Father, and from the Spirit, Jesus Christ our Lord, Amen.

I am Dear Sir, Your Brother in the Gospel,

THOMAS SHAW

Barnsley, England, April 21, 1835.

This Mr. Hewet did not obey the gospel, neither would he investigate the matter. Thus ended the mission of Mr. Hewett.

About the first of July, 1835, there came a man having four Egyptian Mummies, exhibiting them for curiosities, which was a wonder indeed, having also some words connected with them which were found deposited with the mummies, but there being no one skilled in the Egyptian language therefore could not translate the record. After this exhibition Joseph the Seer saw these records and by the revelation of Jesus Christ could translate these records which gave an account of our forefathers, much of which was written by Joseph of Egypt who was sold by his brethren, which when all translated will be a pleasing history and of great value to the Saints.

And now it came to pass while we were yet in the East, there came some letters to the Presidency respecting the Presidency of the elders of Zion, there being some difficulty concerning the matter among them. Therefore the following letter was written to Zion:

KIRTLAND, August 31, 1835.

The Presidency of Kirtland and Zion say that the Lord has manifested by revelation of His Spirit, that the high priests, teachers, priests and deacons, or in other words all the officers in the land of Clay County, Missouri, belonging to the Church are more or less in transgression, because they have not enjoyed the Spirit of God sufficiently to be able to comprehend their duties respecting themselves and the welfare of Zion, thereby having been left to act in a manner that is detrimental to the interest, and also a hindrance to the redemption of Zion.

Now if they will be wise they will humble themselves in a peculiar manner that God may open the eyes of their understanding. It will be clearly manifest that the design and purposes of the Almighty are with regard to them and the children of Zion, that they should let the high council which is appointed of God and ordained for that purpose make and regulate all the affairs of Zion; and that it is the will of God that her children should stand still, and see the salvation of her redemption; and the officers of the Church should go forth, inasmuch as they can leave their families in comfortable circumstances, and gather up the Saints, even the strength of the Lord's house.

And those who cannot go forth conveniently with the will of God, their circumstances preventing them, remain in deep humility; and inasmuch as they do anything confine themselves to teaching the first principles of the gospel, not endeavoring to institute regulations or laws for Zion, without having been appointed of God.

Now we say there is no need of ordaining in Zion, or appointing any more officers, but let all those that are ordained magnify themselves before the Lord by going into the vineyard and cleansing their garments from the blood of this generation. It is one thing to be ordained to preach the gospel, and to push the poeple together to Zion, and it is another thing to be anointed to lay the foundation and build up the city of Zion, and execute her laws. Therefore it is certain that many of the elders have come under great condemnation in endeavoring to steady the Ark of God in a place where they have not been sent.

The high council and bishop's court have been established to do the business of Zion, and her children are not bound to acknowledge any of those who feel disposed to run to Zion and set themselves to be their rulers. Let not her children be duped in this way, but let them prove those who say they are apostles, and are not. The elders have no right to regulate Zion, but they have a right to preach the gospel. They will all do well to repent and humble themselves, and all the Church, and also we ourselves receive the admonition, and do now endeavor and pray to this end.

When the children of Zion are strangers in a strange land, their harps must be hung upon the willows; and they cannot sing the songs of Zion; but should mourn and not dance. Therefore, brethren, it remains for all such to be exercised with prayer, and continual supplication, until Zion is redeemed. We realize the situation that all the brethren and sisters must be in, being deprived of their spiritual privileges which are enjoyed by those who sit in heavenly places in Christ Jesus, where there are no mobs to rise up and bind their consciences. Nevertheless it is wisdom that the Church should make but little or no stir in that region, and cause as little excitement as possible and endure their afflictions patiently until the time appointed, and the governor of Missouri fulfills his promise in settling the Church over upon their own lands.

We would suggest an idea that it would be wisdom for all the members of the Church on the return of the bishop, to make known to him their names, place residence, etc., that it may be known where they all are when the governor shall give directions for you to be set over on your lands.

Again it is the will of the Lord that the Church should attend to their communion on the Sabbath Day, and let them remember the commandment which says, "Talk not of Judgement." We are commanded not to give the children's bread unto the dogs, neither cast our pearls before swine, lest they trample them under their feet, and turn again and rend you. Therefore let us be wise in all things and keep all the commandments of God, that our salvation may be sure, having our armor ready and prepared against the time appointed, and having on the whole armor of righteousness, we may be able to stand in that trying day. We say also that if there are any doors open for the elders to preach the first principles of the gospel, let them not keep silence. Rail not against the sects, neither talk against their tenets, but preach Christ and him crucified, love to God and love to man, observing always to make mention of our Republican principles, thereby if possible we may allay the prejudice of the people. Be meek and lowly of heart, and the Lord of God of our Fathers shall be with you forevermore, amen.

Sanctioned and signed by the presidents:

JOSEPH SMITH, JR. OLIVER COWDERY, SIDNEY RIGDON, F. G. WILLIAMS, W. W. PHELPS, JOHN WHITMER.

P. S. Bro. Hezekiah Peck,

We remember your family with all the first families of the Church who first embraced the truth. We remember your losses and sorrows. Our first ties are not broken; we participate with you in the evil as well as the good, in the sorrows as well as the joys. Our union we trust is stronger than death, and shall never be severed. Remember us unto all who believe in the fullness of the gospel of our Lord and Savior Jesus Christ. We hereby authorize you, Hezekiah Peck, our beloved brother to read this epistle and communicate it unto all the brotherhood in all that region of country.

Dictated by me your unworthy brother, and fellow laborer in the testimony of the Book of Mormon. Signed by my own hand in the token of the everlasting covenant.

JOSEPH SMITH, JR.

74

CHAPTER 17

And it came to pass on the twenty-fourth day of September, 1835, on which day we met in counsel at the house of J. Smith, Jr., the Seer, where we according to a previous commandment given, appointed David Whitmer, captain of the Lord's Host, and Presidents F. G. Williams and Sidney Rigdon his assistants; and President W. W. Phelps, myself and John Corrill, as an assistant quorum, and Joseph Smith, Jr., the Seer, to stand at the head and be assisted by Hyrum Smith and Oliver Cowdery. This much for the war department, by revelation.

October 18, 1835, Sabbath.

This day assembled in the House of the Lord as usual, and the Spirit of the Lord descended upon J. Smith, Jr., the Seer, and he prophesied saying, "The Lord has showed to me this day by the spirit of revelation that the distress and sickness that has heretofore prevailed among the children of Zion will be mitigated from this time forth.

And it came to pass that some of the first elders or presidents of the Church received a prophetic blessing by revelation through the means prepared in the last days to receive the word of the Lord, J. Smith, Jr. Therefore Joseph dictated blessings for himself, Hyrum Smith, Sidney Rigdon, F. G. Williams, Oliver Cowdery, David Whitmer, W. W. Phelps, and myself, as you will find recorded in the Patriarchal blessing book in Kirtland, Ohio, Book A, pages---.

On the sixth day of January, 1836, the elders from Zion who were at Kirtland, Ohio, met to fill vacancies which happened in the high council in Zion in consequence of filling other stations.

Therefore appointed: E. H. Graves instead of P. P. Pratt; Jesse Hitchcock instead of W. E. McLellin; G. M. Hinkle instead of Orson Pratt; Elias Higbee instead of T. B. Marsh.

The Hebrew School commenced January 4, 1836, taught by Seixas.

The first elders attended this school.

Now the time drew near when the Lord would endow his servants, and before he could do this we must perform all the ordinances that are instituted in his house. There was one ordinance, viz, the washing of feet, that we had not yet observed but did perform it according to revelation, which belongs only to ordained members and not the whole Church.

For particulars read the private history of Joseph the Seer.

After this washing of feet came the anointing with holy oil, which was performed by Joseph Smith Senior among the presidents, then the presidents of each quorum proceed to anoint the members thereof, in their proper time and place.

On the 11th of March, 1836, held a council in which Edward Partridge, I. Morley, John Corrill, and W. W. Phelps were appointed wise men and were sent to Missouri with some money to purchase land for the Saints, to seek a place for them.

CHAPTER 18

KIRTLAND, March 27, 1836.

Previous notice having been given, the Church of Latter-day Saints met in the House of the Lord, etc.

See Messenger and Advocate printed at this place for a full statement of the order, sermon, etc., of the dedication of the House of the Lord, published in the March number commencing on page 74 and ending on page 283 inclusive.

CHAPTER 19

And it came to pass that E. Partridge, Isaac Morley, John Corrill, and W. W. Phelps left Kirtland to fill their mission in Missouri, where they had left their families.

They arrived in Missouri in safety. But as soon as these men arrived at home the devil roared in this land and stirred the old Jackson County mob up to great anger, and the people in Clay County. The aforementioned brethren went in search of a place where the Church could settle in peace and found a country north of Ray County that would answer the purpose, providing the few scattered inhabitants that resided there were willing for the brethren to move there and enjoy their religion and constitutional rights, as well as the counties round about.

This move gave great uneasiness and the people of Clay County convened and some were determined to drive the brethren from the state; others were opposed, and finally we succeeded to get the consent of the people of Clay County and a majority of Ray to move into this place now Caldwell County.

Therefore commenced settling this place, Far West, in the summer of 1836; in August the first building was erected.

Some difficulties arose in the land of Kirtland, and dissensions took place which is to be feared will end in the misery of some precious souls.

Some difficulties have taken place in this county, Caldwell, but are now all settled to the satisfaction of all parties as I believe.

T. B. Marsh and D. W. Patton have left for Kirtland, Ohio, to fill a mission in their apostolic capacity.

In the fall of 1838 (i.e., 1837) Joseph Smith, Jr., Sidney Rigdon came to Zion, on a visit to prepare a place for themselves and families.

The situation of the Church both here and in Kirtland is in an unpleasant situation in consequence of the reorganization of its authorities, which was not satisfactory to all concerned. And has terminated in the expulsion of some members, as also some temporal movements, have not proved satisfactory to all parties has also terminated in the expulsion of many members (lines have been drawn across the following words:) among whom is W. W. Phelps and myself. Therefore, I close the history of the Church of Latter-day Saints, hoping that I may be forgiven of my faults, and my sins be blotted out and in the last day be saved in the Kingdom of God, notwithstanding my private situation, which I hope will soon be bettered and I find favor in the eyes of God, all men and his Saints. Farewell. March 1838.

www.ingramcontent.com/pod-product-compliance
Lightning Source LLC
LaVergne TN
LVHW041635070426
835507LV00008B/637